Managing On Nil Every Year

Your Financial Life Matters

Written by Barbara Anderson

Managing On Nil Every Year

Managing On Nil Every Year

In association with

Managing On Nil Every Year

Managing On Nil Every Year

Published in London by Peaches Publications, 2016.
www.peachespublications.weebly.com

The moral right of the author has been asserted.

All rights reserved. No part of this book may be reproduced, stored in a retrieval system, or transmitted in any form or by any means, electronic, mechanical, photocopying, recording, public performances or otherwise, without written permission of the publisher, except for brief quotations embodied in critical articles or reviews. The workbook is for personal use only, commercial use is prohibited unless written permission and a license is obtained from the author; Barbara Anderson.

The right of Barbara Anderson to be identified as the author of this work has been asserted in accordance with sections 77 and 78 of the copyright Designs and Patents Act 1988.

This book is an autobiography. Places and people mentioned are true to the Authors recollection. Some people's names have been changed for confidentially reasons.

Text Copyright © 2016 by Barbara Anderson
www.barbaraanderson.net

British Library Cataloguing in Publication Data: A catalogue record for this book is available from the British Library.

ISBN: 978-1-326-59820-4

Book cover design: Stephen Essel.

Book cover photograph: Winsome Duncan.

Typesetter: Winsome Duncan.

Are You A Winner?

Winners win because they believe a little bit more,

they do a little bit more and when the chips are down,

they push a little bit more and when all seem hopeless they fight a little bit more!

Winning starts in the heart and manifests itself in our actions!

Go win big today for you and your family!

_____

As you win send me an email
Barbara@barbaraanderson.net

Managing On Nil Every Year

Contents

Acknowledgements
Introduction
About The Book
Foreword By Jeff Lestz

Chapter 1 Savings..
Is it a rainy day money or what?
The Rule of 72
15 Annual Equivalent Rate (AER)
What choices do you have?

Chapter 2 Investments..
So what I do with my money then?
Going for broke or going for goals
Risk v Return
Types of Investments

Chapter 3 Protection.. ....
Who provides for the provider?
Types of protection
Watch out for the holes
Other types of personal protection

Chapter 4 Borrowings..
Is it even your money anyway?
50 Types of Mortgages

Chapter 5 Debt Solutions..
What is the solution?

Practice of good habits

Chapter 6 Good Financial Habits………………………………………..
Divide your Income
Entrepreneurial Ideas
Manage automatic payments from your account

Chapter 7 Wills And Trusts……………………………………………….
Protecting You Assets
Do you realize that only 30% of people in the UK have a Will?
Trusts

Chapter 8 The Watchmen…………………………………………………
The main objectives of the FCA
Financial Services Compensation Scheme

Final Word……………………………………….
About the Author……………………………..
Book Barbara to Speak……………………..
References……………………………………….
Recommended Resources…………………
Notes………………………………………………

Acknowledgements

What is more important in life than family?

I want to thank my Mom for the indomitable spirit of standing up and fighting whatever you face in life. The best daughter (in the whole world) Carrel, who has put up with her Mom (from the age of three) going out and building a business sometimes seven days a week and most evenings, and never complains. My brother Craig and sister Melissa for always being supportive.

A special thanks to Alex Gordon and the Dream Success family who first got me to sit down, put pen to paper, and kept up with me the whole way.

To Winsome Duncan and Peaches Publications, thanks for keeping me focused to get the second edition out.

To the best mentors anyone could ask for, my two CEO's at Genistar, Jeff Lestz and Bob Safford Jr who I aspire to be more like every day. To all my colleagues and the Team Ambassadors family, I want to thank you for allowing me to sow into your lives.

To all my other friends and family who have fed into my life in some way shape or form, you are all special. Friends are the people who walk in when the rest of the world walk out.

Introduction

Have you heard the saying, "A fool and his money will soon be parted" Well, today money departs before it even arrives. Or how about "Money Talks?" Well, money doesn't talk, it just goes without saying.

I once heard a wise man say, "If you motivate a fool you will get a motivated fool". However, I also believe if you can motivate a man he could change his community; but if you educate a community, you could change a generation.

Now I am neither calling you a fool nor am I saying that you are uneducated but you have to admit, all of us are ignorant in some areas of our lives and on some issues. Therefore, arming ourselves with some level of awareness and understanding can uncomplicate some of our challenges.

Robert Kiyosaki, one of the world's leading advocates for financial independence and renowned author of 'Rich Dad Poor Dad' said,

"The main reason people struggle financially is because they have spent years in school but learned nothing about money. The result is that people learn to work for money… but never learn to have money work for them."

Whether or not you like talking about money or even like money for that matter, you have little chance of thriving or even surviving without it. Some of your discords with money are inbred, I would even go as far as saying inherited – remember, "money doesn't grow on trees" the common answer from your parents which was sometimes their inability to find the money to give you something you wanted so badly. Now, that was what their parents told them as a child and their parents before and generation after generation have used it as a get out route. Some discords however are bad habits you learn or pick up – try, "keeping up with the Joneses". How do you know how much money the Joneses inherited or how much debt the Joneses are in, to maintain their lifestyle? You don't know. How about understanding how money works and living a comfortable lifestyle that you can maintain? It's amazing how much more value people place on things they earn through hard work compared to those that come seemingly easily.

By this I mean, the money you have to work hard to earn to pay for something, rather than paying for the same item on your credit or store card. Oh, the lovely people who changed that horrible word 'debt' to that nice sounding word 'credit'.

The greatest key to securing a solid financial future is having a Game Plan in place, and then taking the right steps to get there. A Game Plan is a written action plan that takes you through the various actions you need to take to move you from your current situation to the ideal financial situation you would like to be in.

Having helped hundreds of families to put their Financial Game Plan together it never ceases to amaze me when I see the light in their eyes at the possibility of achieving their goals.

Here are 5 steps to get you on track:

Step 1

The first step is to make sure you are adequately protected. In other words, "rent wealth until you create wealth". This is very important as, if anything were to happen to you and knock you off course while you are building your future, your family would not suffer. Even if you do not have dependents, your standard of living could be adversely affected by a change in your health or your ability to bring in an income. I am a great advocate for insurance as, over the years that I have worked in the Financial Services sector, I have seen the positive impact of having protection in place and the negative impact of not having protection.

Step 2

Take charge of your debts and try to clear them in the shortest possible time. This will give you the freedom to build on the other areas of your finances.

Step 3

Be in control of your expenses and see in what areas you can reduce spending. It might be that daily snack or coffee. For instance, if you spend £4 per day on a cup of coffee going to work in an average 20 working day month, you would have spent £80. Wow! Expensive or what? Chances are you make equally good coffee - if not - get better at making coffee. So, you like the paper cup. Buy a box at the Wholesaler. You will still save money.

Step 4

Start saving by using the monies you recover from a better spending habit. Do you realise that if you invested the £80 monthly that you were spending on coffee, at a fixed rate of 6%, at the end of the year you would have accumulated £986.84 and after 5 years, £5581.60.

Step 5

Build additional income streams. Bear in mind if all your income comes from one source you are setting up yourself to always be broke.

> *"The quickest way to double your money is to fold it over and put it in your back pocket."*
>
> **Will Rogers – Humorist, Actor & Social Commentator**

About The Book

The Financial Conduct Authority (FCA), the sole regulator of financial services in the UK, has certain aims and objectives, one of which is to promote public understanding of financial services.

However, there are just so many products - some with names that sound like your sister's, which, when you talk about them, people wonder if you are talking about your sister. Yes! Remember TESSA?

Whilst this is not a comprehensive guide to Financial Services which is such a large area, it offers some insight into some of the basic areas of pitfalls we should avoid in our finances.

After years of educating families on financial matters and trying to de-mystify money for individuals and families, I have tried to cover some of the questions I get from clients and some of the areas they are struggling to try and understand and to allay some of the fears about finances.

I know that money fears can influence lives in a negative way. However, not dealing with your fears does not mean they will go away, it only means they are hidden, ready to surface at the most inopportune time.

Most fears are born out of a lack of knowledge rather than the actual situation one finds themself in. My desire for you is that you will get enough Financial Education from this book so that you can create the financial future you aspire to.

> *"Money isn't everything but it ranks right up there next to oxygen"*
>
> **Zig Ziglar – Motivational Speaker & Author**

Foreword

By Jeff Lestz

I have been coaching and mentoring people for over 30 years and Barbara Anderson is in the top 10 most coachable and enthusiastic people I know.

Barbara possesses 'infectious enthusiasm' and you can see her passion to want to help others achieve their financial goals. From the moment you meet her and see that big smile you know you are in the presence of someone special. She is not only a respected business colleague but I count her as a true friend.

I have total respect for her mental toughness and approach to life. She is one tough lady and I wish there were more people in the world like Barbara Anderson.

In her book, 'manage on nil every year' Barbara gives you a look into the financial world. She educates and challenges you to become more astute with your finances and to take charge of your financial future.

I hope you pour yourself a cup of tea and sit down for a few hours and read Manage On Nil Every Year. It is a great little book designed to help anyone on their journey to financial freedom. Enjoy.

Background

Jeff Lestz was born into a Jewish family but knew what it was like to suffer financial lack when he was orphaned at the young age of 7 after his father committed suicide due to his financial troubles, 2 years later his mother died after a breakdown and a bout of alcoholism.

After moving from an orphanage and to several foster homes he ran away and started living on the streets of Chicago from the age of 12. At aged 15 Jeff's life took a dramatic turn when he accepted the Lord in his life and a mentor took him into his home. Jeff remembers praying for a way out of financial lack and making a commitment that if he ever had money he would spend his life teaching others how to do the same. By the time he was 31 he was a Millionaire and a Multimillionaire by 40 and as fate would have it he has devoted his life to teaching others how to become financially independent.

Jeff is currently the Co-CEO of Genistar Ltd that provides financial services and teaches financial education in the UK and across the world. He presently lives with his wife in Nice, France and doubles up with work life from his UK base in Surrey. When Jeff is not in Nice he usually has a crammed schedule travelling across UK and Europe teaching financial education to groups, speaking at seminars and is in heavy demand as a guest Speaker at Churches and on Radio. www.jefflestz.co.uk

Jeff Lestz

Co-Ceo of Genistar Ltd

Wine makes merry, a feast is for laughter but money is the answer to all things

**Ecl 10 V 19
(The Bible)**

Chapter One

Savings

Savings

"The actions you take today can greatly enhance or alter your future"

Is it A Rainy Day Money or What?

So, everyone wants to put away money for his or her future or a "rainy day" as we call it and sure enough it rains (or seem to) every day in London. Well, do you even know what to do with it or where to keep it so it stays dry and out of the rain?

When you can put money away for it to grow at a great interest rate, then you get to see money at work. If you then allow that money to compound on itself then money truly starts to work for you.

See Money at Work

"Compound interest is the eighth wonder of the world. He who understands it, earns it … he who doesn't pays it." — Albert Einstein

What is Compound Interest?

Simply put Compound Interest is where interest is added to money and that interest stays on the money and accumulates further interest.

Our money is affected by inflation

On the other hand, our money is equally affected by inflation. Inflation being the change in price/value of an item compared to different times or period, which then impacts the spending power of your money.

Looking now at savings, remember that thing you always wanted as a youngster and put away all your pennies so you could buy it (and some managed to put aside enough to get it and some didn't)? Now, that is called **savings**. Savings is the money that you put away short term to pay for things such as holidays, cars etc.

Savings is the money that you put away short term - Savings can be done with most local financial institutions i.e. Banks, Building Societies, Credit Unions, Post Offices and now most leading supermarkets. There are various types of savings accounts such as Instant Access, Notice, Regular Savings, ISAs and Bonds.

The Rule of 72

Having said that - have you ever wondered how long it will take your money to double when you put it in your account? Most people have no idea. So, that been said, have you ever heard of the **Rule of 72**? I was amazed by the Rule of 72 and the fact that they never taught it to us in school.

How long it takes for money to double

Well, here is the Rule of 72 – it is simply the way you work out how long it takes for money to double when you put it away at a given rate of interest. You work this out by dividing 72 by the rate of interest you are given on your money and "abracadabra" your number of years. So, for example if you have £10, you put it in your savings account, and your Bank offers you 2%

then: (72 ÷ 2 = 36) - therefore your £10 will take 36 years to become £20 at 2%.

Add 36 years to your current age

So, let's have a bit of fun on a very serious subject. If you add 36 years to your current age, how old would that make you? Can you imagine how wealthy you would be in 36 years' time with your £20?

When you walk into a financial institution they always seem to have terms and jargons, which, unless you are schooled in finances, can throw you off even with your dictionary.

Here's one that always seem to be by your savings account: AER

Savings Account (and current accounts with a credit balance) pay a rate of interest known as Annual Equivalent Rate (AER). **An Annual Equivalent Rate (AER)** is quoted on savings accounts and current accounts when your balance is in credit. The AER shows how much interest you will earn over the course of a year and takes into account how often the interest is paid and how Compound Interest will affect your money.

Compare how much you will earn on an account

This allows you to compare how much you will earn on an account where interest is paid monthly to one where interest is paid annually.

AERs allow you to compare accounts and work out where your savings will earn the most interest.

The gross rate paid on an account offering monthly interest may be lower than the gross rate on an account offering only one interest payment a year, but when interest is compounded, it may offer higher returns than the latter account.

Example: An account offering a rate of 6.25% paid annually may look more attractive than an account paying 6.12% with monthly interest payments. However, the **AER** on the monthly account is 6.29%, as opposed to an **AER** of 6.25% on the account with annual interest payments.

If there is a charge for withdrawing your money, the **AER** will take this into account - so, for example - if you are charged 30 days' interest for a withdrawal, this will be reflected in the **AER**.

What Choices Do You Have?

If you walk down any High Street you can be easily overwhelmed by the various types of Savings Accounts on offer by different providers. I decided to take this test myself and pulled together some of the ones I encountered.

A Number of Your Saving Options

Instant Access is as the name suggests – instant access to your money with the only restriction possibly being the bank or branch daily cash limit. However, outside of these limits an advance request could ensure the funds are available for your visit to your Financial Institution.

Withdrawals on these accounts are sometimes restricted

Regular Savings are usually accounts where regular deposit periods are set for the account usually with a set amount monthly. However, withdrawals on these accounts are sometimes restricted and can incur withdrawal penalties or interest loss.

Notice Accounts are in fact the opposite of instant access accounts and means you have to give notice based on the period outlined when the account was opened. E.g. a 30-day notice period to withdraw funds.

Bonds are fixed period savings where funds are put away for a fixed time at a fixed rate of interest. These accounts can usually be for periods of days, months or years. Generally, these accounts do not offer access and if the bond period is broken then there is an interest penalty, although in most cases, access is not granted until the bond expires.

ISA is a like a wrapper around an account

Individual Savings Accounts, yes your **ISAs**. Now an **ISA** in itself is not an account but the **ISA** is a like a wrapper around an account that makes it tax-efficient. In other words, the interest that is generated from the account is earned tax-free. Each tax year (i.e. April 6 to April 5), the government gives an allowance for the amount that an individual can save or invest each year where the interest is non-taxable.

How an ISA works

Here is how an **ISA** works. You are allowed to put away funds up to your maximum allowance each tax year, the rules though are any monies withdrawn cannot be replaced. However, in April 2016 ISA Providers were allowed to start offering a Flexible ISA that offers a withdrawal and replacement of funds in the account within the same Tax Year. Bear in mind that it's up to the Provider to offer this and currently not all ISAs provide this option.

Lack of access to funds in an ISA is not necessarily a feature of an ISA but something that a particular Financial Institution may add to that account to restrict movement of funds by the account holder.

Inflation can consume the value of your money
Whilst I am an advocate for savings, remember though that leaving your money in a savings account for a long period of time means that inflation can erode the value of your money. So leaving your life savings in a savings account is not always cost effective.

Whenever I query people why leave their money in a savings account most of them say the same thing, 'it is safe'.

Let me give you my scenario of what safety means:

Example: You have £1000 and you put it in a savings account and you get 4%; here is what it could look like:–

Deposit = £1000

Interest (at 4%) £40 - less Tax at (20%) £8   = £32

Total (in account)   = £1032

Less assumed inflation at 3.5% (£1032x 3.5%) =

                                           (£36.12)

True value   = £995.88

That is an overall loss of £4.12 (£1,000 - £995.88) so, in other words, that is going broke in a safe manner.

Reflection Points

Stop at this point and review last year's Bank Statements. You might even know the answer without looking.

How much interest did you earn on your Savings Account?

....

Then again, how much did it cost you in interest for your overdraft on your Current Account?

So, is your money working for you or someone else?

Interest On Savings

Less

Interest on Overdraft

=

?

Did you recognise all the transactions on your bank statements?

....

If not, why?

....

Are there any additional charges on your bank statements?

....

Money is neither good nor bad it just enhances its owner's character.

Barbara Anderson
Financial Coach and Author

Chapter Two

Investments

Investments

So what do I do with my money then'?

You might be considering, 'what do I do with my money then'? Well, how about Investments?

Investments are monies that you put away for your medium to long-term future. These are monies that are generally placed in more risky, less accessible accounts with the possibility of higher returns on these accounts.

Averaged 15% per annum

Some time ago I was speaking with one of my clients I had assisted in setting up a £50 per month investment to build an education fund for her son. She could not contain her excitement as she told me her investments had averaged 15% per annum. Now, is that fantastic or what? To top it, all of my guidance was free. However, remember, past performance is not a guide to future performance.

Having an Emergency Fund

Your first point of consideration when thinking about investing is having an Emergency Fund. One of the worst things you can do is to put all your money in an Investment Plan and then have to turn to your Investment if you have an emergency.

Most people do not sell their houses or their cars if they have an emergency need. Hence, you should not even consider selling your investment if you have an emergency.

Going for Broke or going for Goals?

When you think about your financial goals for the future you have got to think about the growth of your money and the effects of inflation on your money. Hence, Investments are more favourable for the wise investor.

One of the biggest reasons I find people do not invest is a lack of understanding of Investments. People worry about the stock market crashing and losing their monies but wise spreading of monies in things such as Managed Funds (which I will cover later) is one such way.

Now, that is not to say there aren't any risks associated with investing, of course there are but, if you understand the risks, then you can manage your expectations.

What is the likelihood of everyone stopping their eating, or everyone stopping their travelling, or people stop getting sick, or even, people stop wearing clothes or stop needing shelter?

I could go on with more 'what ifs' but what's the chance of those things happening then; I guess it's about the same possibility of the entire Stock Market being wiped out.

Would you go into panic mode and sell as house prices are declining?

So think about this – if you owned a property in 2005 and you had it valued at £200,000 and then in 2010 due to market conditions it was revalued at a reduced figure of £175,000, would you go into panic mode and sell as house prices are declining?

I am pretty sure I know your answer – it is a resounding 'NO'. So, why if you have money in an investment fund and you are told that the market is down you would sell your investment?

So not selling your house when house prices are down means you do not lose any money (and you can wait until the market bounces back at which point you can sell your house for a profit).

The flip side of that is that if the housing market is booming and you do not sell your house then equally you do not make any money. So the principle is the same as the house as it is an asset. Remember, you only make or lose money if you sell.

You need to understand risk versus returns as your levels of returns (interest) depends on how you feel about risk. The below chart shows you how risk versus returns and ultimately what you can get on your investments.

Looking at the diagram below you will see that Bank Accounts carry the

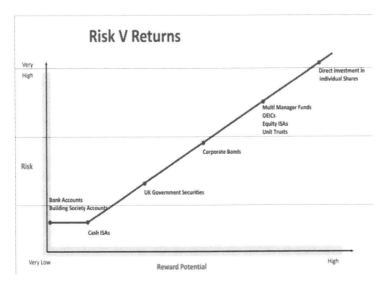

lowest risk but also the lowest returns whilst direct investments in shares carries the highest risk but at the same time carries the highest potential returns.

Types of Investments

Let us now discuss some of the types of investments you have on offer:

As well as our Cash ISAs, we also have stocks and shares. An Investment ISA has the same rules as a Cash ISA but double the allowance. However, the funds are not usually as accessible as a Cash ISA as they are usually linked to the stock market. Whilst there is some level of risk to this type of investment the returns on investment has the potential to be better than on Cash ISAs.

Government Bonds

Government Bonds are another form of Investments. These are also called Gilt Edged or Gilts (the name derived from the gold rim that was placed around the edge of certificates). The funds are usually monies borrowed by the Government for a pre-set/fixed time and interest rate.

They are issued on a Promissory Note i.e. a promise to pay any monies back at a set date in the future and at a fixed rate of interest. As with any monies lent to someone there is always the risk that they will not pay you back. However, this is one of the few investments where you can sleep a bit easier when you are part of it, as the Government has never defaulted on a Bond payment.

Whilst you cannot just withdraw your monies, you can leave the investment by selling to someone else on the open market. Now, the returns on your investment, if you sell, will depend on the market condition at the time you sell, so you may get back more and in some cases, less than you originally invested.

Corporate Bonds

Like the Government when companies sometimes need to raise monies for expansion, instead of issuing new shares, they issue bonds known as Corporate Bonds to raise the funds they require.

Buying a Bond is like lending money to a Company on an IOU. Corporate Bonds however are a lot riskier than Government Bonds as the chance of default is a lot higher. Likewise, the potential return is greater.

The interest paid by the Bond is known as a coupon. The coupon is usually a percentage of the Bond so for e.g. a Bond of £5000 with a 10% coupon will pay you £500 every year and at the end of the period you get back your original investment.

Managed Funds

Imagine this as a pool that you have in the community and you all wanted the pool filled for the kids to play in. If all the people came together and brought a bucket of water then it would be filled a lot quicker. On your own, your bucket of water doesn't have the same power to fill the pool as quickly for the kids to enjoy but by joining forces and pooling resources you can accomplish growth a lot quicker, as your costs will be a lot less.

"Two ox joined together can pull more than the total of the two pulling individually."

Imagine then, there comes extremely hot weather and some of the water evaporates and, at the same time, you decided you wanted your share of water out as you prefer to have your kids playing in your back garden; you will find that you will not get back a full bucket as some of it would have evaporated.

On the other hand, if there were torrential downpours the outcome would be different, as you might need extra buckets for your share. Your sole investment on its own does not have the same impact as your monies pooled with the other investors where your money has a greater bargaining power, so hence can grow larger and faster.

Investments may be a lump sum or through monthly investments. The monies are directly invested with an Investment Company, which also means there is no middleman to pay.

Shares

Shares are single units of ownership in a company. So if you own even one single share in a company that makes you a shareholder in that company and entitles you to share in profits distributed to shareholders by the company. **You do not get interest on your money, instead you get Dividends.**

This also means that if the company goes 'bust' you as a shareholder gets paid out last i.e. after all Creditors are paid so you might not get back your investment. However, as a shareholder in a Limited Company you are not responsible for any of the company's debts. There are two types of shares in a company, Preference (Preferred) Shares and Ordinary Shares.

Preference Shares

Preference Shares are more like monies owed to you by the company. In the event of winding up, payments are made to Preference Shareholders before Ordinary Shareholders. They carry no voting rights but in some cases may carry an option to convert to Ordinary Shares. The Dividends on Preference Shares are fixed and will continue to accrue if not paid on time.

The prices at which Ordinary Shares trade has nothing to do with the par value (the price they were valued at when the company was incorporated and cannot fall below) but are based instead on market conditions. Hence, price fluctuates up and down with market trends.

Investing in shares forms one of the riskiest types of investment, however by the same token, it has the potential for bringing in the greatest return on investment. If you understand the implication of the risks involved then you can find investing in the Stock Market very worthwhile.

Child Trust Fund (Discontinued)

The Child Trust Fund is no longer available to young children as the Government discontinued it, however some of you might still have one and

I believe we should have a look at it. It is a long-term tax-free savings account for children born between 1 September 2002 and 2 January 2011. Your child is entitled to an account only if all of the following apply:

- your child was born between 1 September 2002 and 2 January 2011

- you were paid Child Benefit for that child for at least one day before 4 January 2011

- your child lives in the UK

- your child is not subject to any immigration restriction

The Child Trust was an initiative by the Government to encourage parents to save for their kids future (this has now been discontinued). Children who were entitled to a voucher were given either £500 or £250 by the Government as the initial investment. However there's no access to funds until the child's 18th birthday at which time the funds will be paid over to the child. Any interest earned on funds deposited will be paid tax free.

For children not entitled to a Child Trust Fund there are other forms of tax free savings which we will now cover.

Junior ISAs

This is another form of tax free savings account for children unlike the Child Trust Fund, however, the Government does not make a contribution. A child can have a Junior ISA if they:

• are under 18

• live in the UK

• are not entitled to a Child Trust Fund (CTF) account

Previously a child could not have a Junior ISA if they already have a CTF account. However the government has changed the rules to allow a child trust fund to be transferred to a junior ISA. Children aged 16 could choose to open an adult cash ISA as well as a Junior ISA.

There are two forms of ISAs just like the adult ISAs

There are two forms of ISAs just like the adult ISAs, one being a Cash ISA the other being a Stocks & Shares ISA. Check the allowance with the Inland Revenue HMRC – www.gov.uk/junior-individualsavings-accounts/overview as there are limits to the amount that can be deposited annually. Like the Child Trust Fund the funds are not accessible until the child's 18th birthday at which point he/she can have the funds. If a child is under 16, someone with parental responsibility (for example a parent or step-parent) must open the Junior ISA for that child.

Children aged 16 to 18 can open their own Junior ISA but someone with parental responsibility could still open the account for them. Anyone can make deposits on behalf of the child as long as the annual limit is not exceeded. The Junior ISA will be in the child's name, but the person who opens the account is responsible for managing it. They are called the 'registered contact'. The registered contact is the person who:

- should keep all the paperwork

- reports certain changes of circumstances - for example change of address

- is the only one who can change the account or provider

The provider can change to a different type of Junior ISA or to a different provider at any time. The registered contact can also be changed to someone else with parental responsibility at any time. Interest is payable tax free.

National Savings & Investment (NS&I) Children Bonus

Bonds This is a long-term savings (5 years) for a child under 16 years old until their 21st birthday. Refer to the NS&I website for the limits. The Bond can be cashed in early however, there's no interest paid if cashed in within the 1st year but a bonus is paid at the end of year 5. All returns on investments are paid tax-free. As it is a government backed investment, all deposits are 100% secure.

NS&I Premium

Premium Bonds are accounts that can be opened by anyone over the age of 16 (but may also be opened by Parents/ Guardians/Grand-Parents or Great Grand-Parents for children under 16). Whilst the investments are secure there is no interest paid on investments, instead, the monies that would be used to pay interest are used to fund a monthly prize draw with a £1m jackpot and over 1 million other cash prizes. As this is a tax-free account, any prize monies won would be exempt from tax. This account may be opened Online, by Phone, at the Post Office or by Post.

Savings Certificates Indexed Linked Certificates

These are savings where investments are guaranteed to grow ahead of the Retail Price Index (RPI) (measured inflation each year); your original investment is secure and any interest received is tax-free. There are no penalties to cash in the certificates early but if cashed in within the 1st year then the index linked inflationary interest is not paid.

These investments are not always available as they are only issued at intervals. However, you may register your interest online to be advised of future issues.

This account may be opened Online, by Phone, at the Post Office or by Post.

Fixed Interest Savings Certificates

Unlike the Index Linked Savings Certificates, the Fixed Interest Certificates pay a fixed guaranteed rate of interest for a fixed term. Your original investments are also guaranteed and interest received is tax-free. These Certificates can be cashed in at any time but no interest is paid during the 1st year.

These investments are not always available as they are only issued at intervals. However, you may register your interest online to be advised of future issues.

This account may be opened Online/by Phone/Post Office/by Post.

Guaranteed Growth Bonds

Like the Fixed Interest Certificates, the Guaranteed Growth Bonds pay a fixed interest for a fixed term. Unlike the Fixed Interest Certificates however, the interest earned is taxable. Bonds can be cashed in early but if cashed in early there is a 90-Day penalty interest charged. Therefore, if cashed in within the 1st 90 Days you will get back less than invested.

These investments are not always available as they are only issued at intervals. However, you may register your interest online to be advised of future issues.

This account may only be opened by phone and by post.

Guaranteed Income Bonds

The Guaranteed Income Bonds give you the ability to invest and get a regular monthly income with the rate of interest guaranteed. All interest received is taxable. Bonds can be cashed in early but if cashed in early there is a 90-Day penalty interest charged. Therefore, if cashed in within the 1st 90 Days you will get back less than invested.

These investments are not always available as they are only issued at intervals. However, you may register your interest online to be advised of future issues.

This account may be opened Online/by Phone/Post Office/by Post.

Although some may only be opened either online or by phone.

Guaranteed Equity Bond

The Guaranteed Equity Bond offers you the chance to invest and have your returns linked to the Stock Market (particularly the Financial Times Stock Exchange - FTSE). This means that if the market grows then your investments grow. However, unlike some investments, if the market falls then your original investment is guaranteed.

All returns on investments are taxable. These Bonds cannot be cashed in before the bond matures and closing balance is paid to a Bank Account.

These investments are not always available as they are only issued at intervals. However, you may register your interest online to be advised of future issues.

This account may be opened Online/by Phone/Post Office/by Post.

Reflection Points

Could your money be working harder for you than it is currently doing?

....

Imagine if you had put your money in an investment account as opposed to a savings account, how much more do you believe you could have earned?

....

Does that mean then that you should be putting away your money in a different savings vehicle?

....

"Too many people spend money they earned, to buy things they don't want, to impress people that they don't like".
Will Rogers

Chapter Three

Protection

Protection

"Your family will reap tomorrow what you sow today"

Who provides for the provider?

What would you say is the most valuable asset you have? If you were bound by contract or law to protect something would you protect it? If you had an asset that you believed was valuable and you did not have to protect it would you do it?

Let's use an example here - if you had a brand new Mercedes parked outside your home and there was no law that compelled you to have motor insurance - wouldn't you still worry about it being stolen? How about it being damaged in an accident by someone who could not pay to fix it? Would any of those worry you?

If you knew your IPAD was going to be lost tomorrow, would you insure it today?

If you knew you were going have a fire at your house tomorrow, would you take insurance out today? If you knew you were going to have a serious illness tomorrow, would you get protection today? If your family and you knew you were going to die tomorrow would you protect yourself today? Lots of 'what ifs,' but you have to admit no one has the information at hand to foretell the future and because these are all possibilities you need protection.

How do you know if you have adequate cover?

So you have Life Insurance and yes, you might even have Critical Cover but do you understand your policy? How do you know if you have adequate cover? How can you tell if you have the right amount, the right type, too much or too little cover?

In fact, when you purchased your cover how did you decide on the amount of cover? Was it your decision or someone else's? When you decide to purchase your cover, you should choose based on your needs.

It was with a bittersweet feeling I sat in my office reading a letter from one of our Insurance Providers regarding a client who had a stroke that affected their ability to continue to work. The Provider advised they had accepted the claim and would be making payment to the client. As I read it I could not help but think of all the uninsured people who would suffer if a serious illness occurred and the families who would experience hardship in the event of death.

A rule of thumb in planning your protection is that your income should be provided for at least 10 times your annual income

There are a number of things to consider such as your responsibilities versus dependents, partner, financial commitments such as mortgage and other debts, income replacement for day to day living for family, things such as kids' education, providing for illness and final expenses. So here is a formula to help you calculate your needs:

Debts + Income + Mortgage + Extras = Required Protection

Extra, could be things such as kids' education, funeral expenses. There are various types of protection ranging from Personal Insurances, which insure individuals rather than companies or organisations. General Insurances typically comprises any insurance that is not determined to be life insurance.

UK General Insurance is broadly divided into three areas:

1. Personal - Auto (Private Car), Homeowner (Household), Pet insurance, Creditors insurance and others.

2. Commercial - Employer liability, Public liability, Product liability, Commercial fleet and other general insurance products.

3. London market – such as Supermarket, Football players and other very specific risks.

Make sure you have the right type of protection for your needs.

Disclosure here is just as important as with all the other forms of protection. As always, make sure you have the right type of protection for your needs. For e.g., if you let your property make sure you have Landlord's cover and not Residential Cover because it is cheaper. If your tenant is on Benefits make sure you disclose it, as the premium may be different for Professional Tenants.

Not being honest and upfront could invalidate your claim

Remember also that if you say you have a Burglar Alarm and it is not always on and you are burgled then your claim may be invalidated.

Let us look at Personal Insurances. Life Insurance, Critical Illness, Serious Illness, Personal Accident, Family Income Benefit are all types of Personal Protection. Life Insurance, Critical Illness and Serious Illness Cover falls under two broad headings – Whole of Life or Term Cover.

Whole of Life Cover

Whole of Life Cover is a plan that stays in place until death. Some Whole of Life policies only has an insurance element whilst others have an investment element built in which allows cash in option. With this type of Whole of Life Policy, the premium is generally more expensive as it carries an investment side and it must pay out at some point in the future.

Life cover & investment

For this particular type of Whole of Life Cover you generally pay for two things (life cover & investment) but only ever get one. Therefore, if you cash in your policy you get the investment portion but the life cover ends. Likewise, if you die the life cover pays out and your beneficiary does not get any monies accrued in the investment part of the plan.

Term Life Insurance

Term Insurance is insurance which provides coverage at a fixed rate of payments for a period of time, the relevant term. After that period expires, coverage at the previous rate of premiums is no longer guaranteed. You must at the time either forego coverage or potentially obtain further coverage with different payments or conditions:

• Term insurance is the least expensive way to purchase a substantial death benefit on a coverage amount.

• If you die during the term, the death benefit will be paid to your beneficiary or estate.

• The sum assured pays out if the risk that is covered by the policy occurs during the term, e.g. death or critical illness.

• Payment is made in a one-off lump sum.

• If payment of the sum assured occurs, the policy ceases.

- If the specified risk (i.e. serious illness or death) does not occur during the term, the policy ceases at the end of the term and there is no cash value.

- If the policy is surrendered during the term, it has no cash value.

- The cover ceases and the policy lapses with no cash value, if the premiums are not paid within a certain period after the due date.

Level Cover

Level Cover is one type of term cover.

- The sum assured remains constant throughout the term.

- Level term assurance is often used when a fixed amount is needed on death to repay a debt such as an interest-only mortgage.

- Over the term of the policy, the real value of the sum assured can be affected by inflation. As prices rise, the sum assured remains the same, thus reducing the policy's purchasing power, over its term.

Decreasing Cover

Decreasing Cover is another form of Term Cover

• With Decreasing Term Cover, the sum assured reduces over the term of the policy. This is typically by equal annual amounts.

• The monthly premium does not decrease but remains the same.

• Decreasing Term Cover is normally used to cover a debt that decreases over time, such as a capital repayment mortgage. The policy is usually set up so that it decreases in line with the outstanding debt.

Increasing Term Cover

•With Increasing Term Cover, the sum assured increases each year by a fixed amount or percentage of the original sum assured.

• The advantage of increasing term assurance is that the increases can counter the effects of inflation on the purchasing power of the sum assured.

- For example, if the rate of inflation was 3%, it would mean that prices were rising, on average, by 3% a year, and therefore the real value of the sum assured was decreasing by 3% a year. Increases to the sum assured can be used to offset the effects of inflation. However, as it is difficult to predict what inflation rate will be in the future, increases to the sum assured are not guaranteed to offset the effects of inflation.

Convertible Term Cover

This is a term cover product that includes an option to convert the policy into a whole-of-life or endowment assurance without further evidence of health.

Renewable Term Cover

Renewable Term Cover includes the option to renew the policy at the end of the term for the same sum assured without further medical evidence.

The premium for the new policy is based on your age on exercise of the option.

The premium is typically higher than for a term policy without the option to renew.

Family Income Benefit

Family income benefit is a type of decreasing term policy that provides income on the death of the breadwinner.

It provides income, rather than a lump sum. It pays out tax-free regular income (monthly or quarterly) from the date of the death of the life assured, until the end of the chosen period.

Inheritance Tax is usually paid on an estate when someone dies. It is also sometimes payable on trusts or gifts made during someone's lifetime. Some estates do not have to pay Inheritance Tax if they are valued at less than the threshold. The tax is payable at 40 per cent on the amount over this threshold or 36 per cent if the estate qualifies for a reduced rate as a result of a charitable donation.

Inheritance Tax is due if your estate - including any assets held in trust and gifts made within seven years of death - is valued over the Inheritance Tax threshold

www.hmrc.gov.uk/inheritancetax.

One way of countering Inheritance Tax is to put the policy in trust.

Critical Illness

What would happen to your finances if you were to undergo a major or life-threatening illness? As advances are made in medical care, many people who suffer major life-threatening illnesses, such as heart attacks or strokes, now survive.

However, a large number of these individuals may not be able to continue working and the cost of ongoing (sometimes) specialist treatment may prove quite expensive. The loss of income due to the inability to work following a serious illness is one of the main reasons why it is important to protect yourself from the financial consequences. When a claim is made for a Critical Illness and the claim is paid then the policy ceases.

Serious Illness Cover

A lot of people are familiar with Critical Illness Cover but not as familiar with Serious Illness Cover. They are quite similar but unlike Critical Illness Cover that only pays out on total critical illness occurring, Serious Illness pays out on a wider range of illnesses based on the level of severity. For example Critical Illness Cover would only pay out if you have lost both of your legs whilst Serious Illness Cover would pay out if you have lost one leg. Serious Illness Cover takes into consideration how the occurrence has affected your living.

Serious Illness Cover also offers the option to restore your level of cover to what it was before your illness occurred and you made a claim. So making a claim doesn't necessarily mean the closure of your policy.

The premium for both Critical Illness and Serious Illness Covers are pretty similar, so the cost is not a factor to make a choice.

- Critical Illness or Serious Illness cover provides a lump sum payment on the diagnosis of one of a specified range of Critical Illnesses or Serious Illnesses.

- Whereas life cover may be unsuitable for those with no financial dependents, Critical Illness or Serious Illness cover could be applicable to cover medical costs.

- A common use for Critical Illness/Serious Illness cover is to protect the outstanding amount owed on a mortgage or a large debt. If you suffered a Critical Illness or Serious Illness, and were unable to work as a result, your ability to continue repaying your mortgage or debt could be affected. In this case the lump sum would pay out an amount equal to the cover amount.

- Not being able to work is not a condition for payment of the lump sum: a lump sum will pay out if one of a range of specified critical illnesses is diagnosed.

Critical and Serious Illness Cover can be: Standalone: A term assurance providing protection in the event of the Critical or Serious Illness. It may also be added to:

- another policy

- a term assurance

- an endowment; or

- a whole of life policy

Accidental Death Plan

An Accidental Death Policy is a term plan that has a relatively cheap premium with what seems like a substantial amount of cover, however, this cover will only pay out if you die accidentally or in an accident. In fact the real life cover is only a small amount, and in some cases only a few thousand pounds.

Low-Start policies

What you need to consider is that these policies start off at a lower monthly premium but increase over the term of the policy, so what may start out as a seemingly lower quote might in fact cost more than a level term policy over the whole policy period.

Two life insurance policies may be better than one

Couples can buy a joint policy that covers both lives or can have one policy each. Joint-life policies pay out on either the first partner's death or the second. First-death policies are often used to provide a lump sum for your family if you or your partner dies, for example to pay off a mortgage. Second-death policies can be used to cover an anticipated Inheritance Tax (IHT) bill.

And yet, if you are looking for cover for you and your partner, two single-life policies may offer much better value than a joint-life policy. For a start, two individual policies will often be no more expensive than a joint policy. Also if both partners die within the period covered by the policies, then that's double the payout to their beneficiaries.

Also, as a joint policy ends on the death of one partner, if the surviving partner wanted to take out a new policy in their own name, they would pay more for the cover at that stage as they are older at the outset of the new policy.

An extra benefit is that single-life policies give more flexibility as the payout goes to your estate and is distributed under the terms of your Will. Joint-life policies tend to pay out to the surviving spouse.

Reviewable life insurance policies

If a quote seems unusually low, check if it is a reviewable policy. Rather than the monthly premium staying the same (as would happen with a regular 'guaranteed' policy), the premium is only guaranteed for the first few years (often the first 5 or 10 years), at which time it is re-priced. As prices rise considerably as you get older, you may find that reviewable premiums become unaffordable in later life.

Health issues when buying life insurance

If you withhold any information about your health, your policy could be invalidated and might not pay out. If you have a preexisting medical condition you should still be able to get life cover, but it may cost more and be harder to find.

Whole of Life Policies

You are paying for two things but will only ever get one in return i.e. you have life insurance and investment but you or your beneficiary will only ever get one not both. So a word of wisdom – keep your life cover separate from your investments. You can buy a less expensive Term Cover and the premium difference could be used to start an investment fund.

Other pitfalls - Whenever you buy a life policy to cover a mortgage or a loan make sure it's the right type of cover. So you never buy a decreasing term policy for an interest only mortgage even though it is cheaper; as it is not sufficient for the need.

Other Types of Personal Protection

Relevant Life Policies

A Relevant Life Plan is a tax-efficient life term assurance plan available to employers to provide an individual death in service benefit for an employee (including salaried directors). It is designed to pay a lump sum if the employee dies whilst employed during the length of the policy. It pays out a tax-free, lump sum on the death (or diagnosis of a terminal illness).

Permanent Health Insurance (PHI):

This type of cover provides a replacement income in the event of illness, disability, or accident for the long-term.

Accident Sickness and Unemployment (ASU):

Provides a set payment in return for a specified premium if the insured suffers injury, sickness, or becomes unemployed but is usually for a short term up to about 2 years.

Payment Protection Insurance (PPI)

This type of cover is quite similar to Accident Sickness & Unemployment Cover usually purchased to cover credit commitments such as loans, hire purchases, store cards and credit card payments. The intention of this type of PPI is to cover the monthly payments if you are unable to work due to accident, sickness or unemployment until the debt is repaid or you go back to work, whichever is sooner.

This product works better as a standalone product and not where it is added to the credit commitment, it is meant to cover as interest is added to the cover amount just like another loan.

Private Medical Insurance (PMI):

This type of cover pays the costs of private medical treatment in the event of illness.

Long-term Care Insurance: Covers the costs of nursing care in old age.

Mortgage Payment Protection: Pays the mortgage costs if the client is unable to work because of ill health or redundancy.

Reflection Points

Do you have adequate insurance in place if you were to suffer a major illness or die?

....

Would your family's future be financially secure if you were unable to provide for them?

....

Or, would you be financially ok if something were to happen to you, would you be able to meet your everyday needs?

....

Save More, Spend Less and Financial Freedom will arrive a lot sooner.

Barbara Anderson Financial Coach and Author

Chapter Four

Borrowings

Borrowings

"If you practice good spending habits you can conquer debts"

Is it even your money anyway?

Here are a few more of those annoying abbreviations that constantly shows up when you are borrowing. APR is Annual Percentage Rates and is used as a measure of how much it costs to borrow money and is quoted by mortgage lenders and companies offering personal loans and credit cards. The APR includes any upfront fees charged by the lender, spread over the period for which you are borrowing the money.

It is not always immediately apparent how much you will be paying

When a product provider quotes an interest rate, it is not always immediately apparent how much you will be paying - or be paid - if you take out the product. When shopping around for savings accounts, for example, different providers may choose to quote monthly or annual interest rates, making it difficult to compare accounts fairly.

Some lenders charge hefty upfront fees

When it comes to loans and mortgages, some lenders charge hefty upfront fees, and low interest rates, while others charge low fees and high interest rates.

It gives you an idea of how much your borrowing will cost if you were to remain overdrawn for a whole year

If you are trying to compare accounts, look for the APR, rather than the headline rate.

EAR is quoted when you are borrowing money

Like the APR, an EAR is quoted when you are borrowing money - this time in the form of an overdraft. Unlike an APR, this does not include any fees for going overdrawn. Instead, it gives you an idea of how much your borrowing will cost if you were to remain overdrawn for a whole year.

The calculations take into account the rate of interest being charged, how often it is charged, and the effect of compounding it - charging interest on interest - over the year.

Mortgages

A mortgage is a long-term loan borrowed to purchase a property. So how does it work? You want to buy your own property, where do you want to live? How is your credit rating? This you can check online with a Credit Reference Agency such as Equifax or Experian. The better your Credit Score the better your chances of getting a better mortgage deal.

Based on those findings how much deposit do you have? Have you got adequate funds for your legal fees and stamp duty? When you buy a property in the UK over a certain price, you have to pay Stamp Duty Land Tax (SDLT).

A mortgage is the biggest financial commitment most people will undertake in their lifetime. Speaking with my Coach and Mentor I've learnt an important lesson about taking on a mortgage. A mortgage is the biggest financial commitment most people will undertake in their lifetime, so you come from having some money stashed away in an account to suddenly having this major credit arrangement and no money. You go from being in a positive net worth to negative net worth in one day.

Make sure you always have some money in excess of initial costs

You anticipate being in your own home with baited breath. Suddenly the once beautiful house that you viewed a few months before doesn't seem as beautiful as you notice the carpets need to be replaced, you don't like the bathroom suite and the walls need a coat of paint. Frustrating isn't it? So what do you do at this point?

Types of Mortgages

Borrow some more money or live with it as it is? Make sure you always have some money in excess of initial costs to meet eventualities.

Interest Only Mortgages

This is where you take on a mortgage to purchase a property but the monthly payment covers the interest only. In other words, this is just an expensive way to own and to live in a property. You pay the mortgage, you are responsible for the upkeep of the property for however long the mortgage period is and at the end of that period you have to cough up the original capital borrowed.

For example you borrow £100,000 for 25 years and your interest is 5% and you are paying interest every month of £416.67, you would pay the lender back £125,000 (i.e. £5000 in interest every year for 25 years) over the period and still owe the original £100,000.

Most people do not make additional plans to repay the capital

The sad thing about this is that most people do not make additional plans for repaying the capital and as such have no means of repaying the mortgage after the period expires. Whilst this type of mortgage may be the cheapest in terms of monthly payment it is the most expensive as whatever time you decide to start making payment on the capital any interest payment made up to that point is not taken into consideration.

Anyone who takes an interest only mortgage should make adequate provisions for repayment at the end of the period as there is no guarantee that the lender will issue further funding to continue the mortgage. An investment is one option for meeting the short fall at the end of the mortgage term.

Repayment Mortgages

This type of mortgage, also known as capital and interest mortgage is where you pay, as the name suggests, both the capital and the interest at the same time. So whatever the period the mortgage is over, if payments are maintained then the mortgage will be repaid in the set period.

Mortgage Product (Rates)

Fixed Rates

A fixed rate mortgage is one where the rate is fixed for a set term for e.g. 1 year, 2 years, 3 years or 5 years after which it reverts to another rate, usually the Standard Variable Rate. During the fixed term there is usually an exit penalty so leaving the deal during this period is not advisable.

Standard Variable Rate

This is a rate that is set by each Financial Institution as their basic mortgage rate and as the name suggests, it fluctuates with the movement of the Bank of England's base rate as well as other factors as decided by that Financial Institution.

Tracker

The Tracker rate product is one where the product tracks the Bank of England's base rate and is usually a fixed percentage in excess of the base rate. Hence, if the rate rises or falls the excess remains the same. For example if the base rate is 1% and the tracker is 1% above base rate then the actual rate will be 2%. However if the base rate rises to 1.5% then the new rate will be 2.5%. Likewise if it falls to 0.5% then the rate will become 1.5%

LIBOR

The London Inter-Bank Offer Rate (LIBOR) is the rate at which the banks trade amongst themselves. More often now secondary lenders use this as basis for their lending rates to clients. It is generally higher than the Bank of England's base rate and reduction in the Bank of England's rate is not normally reflected where borrowings were attached to the LIBOR.

LOANS – are short-term borrowings for usually smaller figures than a mortgage.

There are generally two types of loans; these are secured and unsecured loans.

Secured Loans

These loans are usually secured against assets e.g. against properties, land, vehicle or other forms of redeemable assets, i.e. assets that can be taken possession of and resold to pay off the balance of the loans, if not repaid. So a charge against a property (the property could also have a mortgage against it, in which case it is a second charge or Re-Mortgage, in which case it is a first charge) is a secured loan.

Car or vehicle loans (differs to general personal loans taken then used to buy a car) are also secured against the car. So failure to pay could result in the car being repossessed. Secured loans sometimes carry a lower Annual

Percentage Rate (APR) than its counterpart, the unsecured loan.

Unsecured Loans

These are loans that are lent to borrowers with no interest held against an asset as security. These days unsecured loans are not only funded by banks but also by doorstep lenders to pay day loan companies on the high street and online.

An unsecured loan is also known by the name Personal Loan.

Unsecured loans tend to carry a much higher Annual Percentage Rate (APR) than secured loans. Interest rates on secured loans could range from about 5% APR with your High Street Bank to the excess of 4,000% APR with a Pay Day Loan Company.

As the need for quick cash becomes more apparent so has the springing up of Short Term Lenders and Pawnbrokers in every 'nook and cranny'. What seems like quick cash and easy repayment is not true as the true cost is significantly higher.

Credit Cards & Overdrafts

Credit cards like Overdrafts are Revolving Debts. Simply put, any monies owed on the account and not cleared will continue to accrue Debit Interest. So if you owed £100 and your total charges for the month were £5 and you paid (minimum 2.5% on the £100) £2.50, then the following month if you incur another £5 in charges you will now be charged interest on £107.50 (i.e. the original £100 + £2.50 unpaid from last month + this month's £5).

If you do a balance transfer from a card to another card with 0% rate then make sure you clear the balance before the offer ends, as the follow on rate can be quite hefty. Also look out for clauses in the arrangement that can affect you such as a different rate for new purchases on the card.

Overdrafts are now the norm on Current Accounts but even with an approved overdraft this can now be costly as some Banks charge daily for the facility whilst others have a set APR usually in excess of 15% per annum. Think about using your approved overdraft at a cost of £1 per day for a month, that's an average of £30 every month. Just like the Credit Card if you don't clear your overdrawn balance you will have Debit Interest accruing.

How will the rule of 72 affect credit and store card borrowings?

Earlier I mentioned the Rule of 72 and the impact it has on your Savings Account. So, how does it affect your borrowing? If you have a Credit Card with an outstanding balance of £500 and the rate is 24% then 72÷24 is 3. Therefore after 3yrs including what you've paid you would have doubled (negatively) what you started out with. Paying only the minimum on your credit card means you will in most cases never clear the outstanding balance.

Reflection Points

Do have you any Credit or Store Cards?

....

Do you sometimes try and pay a bit extra?

....

Pull your current statement out (depressing I know), what is your balance like? Is your monthly payment making even a dent into the balance?

....

Based on your current borrowings, how soon will it be before you become debt free?

....

Have you heard of debt stacking, where you can reduce your debts in a shorter period?

....

How many Millionaires do you know who became wealthy investing in a Savings Account? I rest my case.

Robert G. Allen – Financier & Author

Managing On Nil Every Year

Chapter Five

Debt Solutions

Debt Solutions

What is the solution?

You do not have to suffer in silence with your financial situation, there are options or as the song goes 'problems have solutions'.

There are various options available to you if you are struggling with debt payments. Let us cover some of your options here:

Token Payment

If you are in a bad financial position you can write to your creditors and explain your situation, especially in cases of ill health and loss of income. Ask them if they could freeze the interests on your accounts and if possible offer a token payment of £1 until your situation improves.

Debt Management Plans (DMP)

A DMP may be considered if you have some money left over monthly after covering your essential needs. This is an arrangement with your creditors to pay back a smaller monthly amount to clear your debts. This is usually done through a Debt Management Company. They will speak directly with your creditors and collect a set monthly amount and distribute it amongst your creditors. Be mindful however that most of these companies charge for the service in the form of an upfront fee, a monthly administration fee or both. There are still companies though that provide a free service.

Administrative Orders

An Administrative Order is possible when you have debts of less than £5000 and also have a County Court Judgement (CCJ). It is decided by the court what is a reasonable amount for you to pay back based on your income. The payment is then made monthly to the court and distributed by the court to your creditors.

Debt Relief Orders (DRO)

In order for you to qualify for a DRO you need to be on a low income, have less than £15,000 of debts and have £50 or less in income per month after paying household expenses. You also need to have no more than £300 in assets or savings or a car that is worth more than £1000. No outstanding fines, court orders or child maintenance payments, student loans or loans from social funds can be included in the order.

The order period ends after 12 months, however you may have a restriction for between 2 years to 15 years on being unable to undertake certain transactions. The cost for a DRO is £90 and can be paid in instalments over 6 months.

Individual Voluntary Arrangements (IVA)

An IVA is a formal arrangement between you and your creditors in relation to your debts and allows you to pay back all or part of your debt over a fixed period of time (usually 5 years). For an IVA to be set up there needs to be in excess of two creditors (more than one debt with the same creditor only counts as one) and you need to have disposable income of £200 per month.

For the arrangement to be put in place creditors owed 75% of the outstanding debts must agree for it to be accepted. If you own your property, you will be asked to raise the outstanding amount if you have equity. If you are unable to raise the funds then the plan will be extended for a further 12 months. The thing to bear in mind here is that an IVA is not for everyone.

Bankruptcy

A bankruptcy can be a last resort if you have no money to pay your creditors or it would take an extremely long time to clear your debts on your income. Once you are bankrupt the debts are written off and you are discharged from the bankruptcy in usually 12 months.

I am seeing so many more people with personal debts in excess of £20,000. In fact I have heard people say they would contemplate suicide. I get calls seven days per week asking for guidance and help with finances. As I work through people's finances with them and direct them to a solution I know exactly what it means to do right by people.

Reflection Points

How are you coping with debts?

....

Are you drowning?

....

Are you too scared to look?

....

Do you want to talk about it?

Let us talk!

Go to: www.barbaraanderson.net

Chapter Six

Good Financial Habits

Divide your Income

Consider dividing up your income when you get it into four areas – Giving, Short Term Savings, Long Term Savings and Spending. In fact you need three accounts, one for your Short Term/Emergency Savings, one for your Long Term/Future Savings and one for your Spending Account.

Start children off with a Passbook account

So they can see their money grow and learn the concept of saving at an early age. Allow them to go into the bank with you and give them the Passbook to give to the cashier so they can see the movement themselves.

Entrepreneurial Ideas

Start teaching your kids from an early age to save, give and spend less than they get but, equally as important, if they have creative ideas build on those ideas and encourage them. Gone are the days when 'you work hard, get a good education, get a good job and retire comfortably'.

The majority of today's millionaires did not inherit their wealth but instead created it and that includes the super-smart Bill Gates.

Pay yourself first

Always divide your income into four – 1st Part (10%) is giving, 2nd Part (10%) is saving for short term goals/emergencies, 3rd Part (10%) for your long term goals and future, 4th Part (70%) your living expenses.

It stands to reason that if you cannot manage on 70% (the chances are you cannot manage on 100% either) you need to increase your income. It is such a fantastic concept that by increasing your income your 10% giving and your 20% saving portions become larger.

Spend less than you earn

To be in an upward financial position you must always spend less than you earn. So get away from overdrafts and credit cards.

Pay your debts off in the shortest period - Try not to be a borrower but if you must borrow, try to repay your debts off in the shortest possible time. Look out for early repayment penalties.

Try saving for purchases instead of borrowing

As the old saying goes, 'a penny saved is a penny earned'. If you take out a mortgage and then later do a re-mortgage then you must **ALWAYS** try to keep the term the same as was remaining on the previous mortgage.

Therefore, if you take your mortgage over 25 years and have 22 years left on your mortgage when you re-mortgage you should start the new mortgage with 22 years.

Look for Savings Plans with Returns where your money actually grows

The combined effects of tax and inflation can make what looks like a favourable return on your money, in fact, be less than favourable. Look for savings or investments where the returns are in excess of the combined total of the tax and inflation. If currently your returns on investment are less than 5% you are certainly not growing your money (as pointed out earlier on – 'remember going broke safely').

Manage Automatic Payments from your Account

Try to have payment arrangements including Direct Debits and Standing Orders come out your account the day you get paid. If this is not possible set up reminders to your phone for a few days before the due date, if you will not have funds in your account then cancel the Payment as incurring a charge for an item that you are still going to have to make is no fun.

In some cases, as well as the Bank Charge, the company involved may make a charge which is charged for the missed payment not the cancelled Payment, hence it's better to be charged once than for both.

Budgeting

It's not always easy to budget especially when prices change weekly at the supermarket. However, list the things that you need and have a figure in mind that you plan to spend that week and walk with a calculator.

Cashless and Cardless

Do not walk with Cash, you have no plans for it apart from losing it, as you suddenly see things that you can spend it on. Have just enough for an emergency. Why not try leaving your cards at home. Remember! "Don't have it, can't use it". Most people will not travel home to get the means to pay for an item and come back and if they do they can have a change of heart on the journey.

Keep your Receipts

Hang on to your receipts as you can change your mind and have your money back. I for one do not like Credit Notes and Gift Cards or my money sitting in someone else's account giving them interest and I am obliged to go back to the same shop.

Cash-back Shopping - If possible use cash-back programs for shopping. There are currently quite a few companies that offer cash-back for shopping with most High Street Stores and Supermarkets. There are also now cards (incl. Debit Cards) that offer cash-back on spending. Then there are **Voucher Codes** which will reduce your bill when you shop online. I was recently buying a pair of school shoes for my daughter in a sale online for £30 and used a voucher code I got online that gave me a further 11% off and a code that gave me free delivery, a total saving of about £8.

Widen your network

If you have a wide Social Network (people who are striving to be better, not the ones who do not uplift you) then you are more likely to hear of deals as people generally love to spread good news. Take me for e.g. I go to the Supermarket and see a box of Washing Powder that was usually £20 being sold for £10 I am on the phone in a jiffy telling my friends and family.

Multiple Income Sources

In a constantly changing environment having only one source of income is very unsafe especially if you are the only one in charge of paying the income, meaning a JOB. Most people shiver at the thought of paying their own income i.e. being in sales, a commission based role or owning their own business. However you can start a home-based business as an additional income source.

In terms of the tax benefit having a business as a secondary income instead of a second job is much more favourably for you. You realise that when you are an employee your tax comes out before it comes into your hands but being Self-Employed or a Business Owner you may claim for your expenses before you pay your tax.

Know what you are entitled to

If you have children claim your Tax Credits. Even working individuals without children can claim Tax Credits. If you live alone claim your Single Person Allowance for your Council Tax.

Make sure your home is adequately insured

It is important to have adequate home insurance cover as not having the right level of cover could leave you out of pocket. You can have adequate cover without paying an arm and a leg.

It is usually hard to tell what is the rebuilding cost for your house, especially when you don't have a surveyor or value coming round every year to assess this amount for you. A useful website to know is

http://abi.bcis.co.uk/calculator/calculator.aspx

Money does not care to whom it belongs, be it in the pocket of paupers or the coffers of Kings.

**Barbara Anderson
Financial Coach and Author**

Chapter Seven

Wills and Trust

Wills and Trust

Protecting your Assets now and for the future or Are You?

So after working hard and accumulating your assets what would you like to happen to these assets? Could it be that you would like your loved ones to one day inherit those assets? Is it that you wish they will inherit, hope they will inherit or know they will inherit. If you do then, great, I am sure you have gotten it all drawn up into a will, Congratulations!!! You are one of only a few savvy ones who have done that.

There are several ways that people leave their lasting instructions, such as Letters of Wishes, Wills and Trusts. Each one plays a different role and can all be combined. We will look at each one separately.

Do you realise that only 30% of people in the UK have a Will? In fact, another 70% of those do not have a sufficiently drawn up will. Scary or What? Guess what? You have a great advantage over these – You my dear are still alive. What is the next best time to get it right? Now!!!

What exactly is a 'Will' then? Simply put – A Will is a document that lays out your instructions of what you would like to happen to your assets when you pass away. If you die without a will then this is termed as 'intestate'. If you don't have a Will or have a valid Will drawn up at the time of your passing, then it's the Court that decides how your Assets are distributed. This might even be contrary to your wishes as those you want to inherit might not and those you don't want just might. For eg, Step-Children, Foster Children, Family Members and Close Friends might be people you want to leave some of your Assets but if it's not written then your wishes won't be honoured.

Here is a scenario:

You are married, you have children, you own some assets, possibly a Property jointly. Unfortunately, you pass away and you have no will so what happens? Great, your partner inherits. Your partner then remarries and still doesn't make a Will then the unfortunate happens again they also pass way. Now what happens? Nothing! Your kids get nothing. They are now step-children to the new surviving Partner and are not entitled to anything. Is this what you expected or expect?

A Will is one of the most important document that your family will need at your passing as not only will it carry out your wishes but it reduces things like family squabbles and allows your Estate to get sorted out more quickly than if you did not have one.

Why having an up-to-date Will is important?

- To specify who gets your Assets
- To say who has responsibility for your children
- Remove people you no longer want to inherit
- Specify Funeral arrangements
- Distribute Properties

- Where you are a Sole Trader ensuring that plans are in place to keep the Business running

Here are a few points you need to take serious note of:

Married Couples – Without a Will

- The Law dictates your Partner gets the first £250,000 of your Estate after all liabilities and outstanding affairs have been settled and then half of anything
- remaining and the other half is what's then divided amongst your children. - A recent example of this was Peaches Geldof who died without a Will. After her Estate was settled there was about £395,000 left after her Husband Thomas Cohen received the first £250, 000, then received a half of the remaining about £195,000 which represented about £97,500 and the remainder of about £97500 was to be split between her two sons Phaedra and Astala.

This was according to the Mail Online on Dec 13, 2015)

Living together – But not married

- Your Partner has no right to your Estate even if you have children together, in fact your Estate might be treated like you are Single.

Single – With no Will

- Your Asset will get divided by the Court.

Childcare Arrangements

- The court and the Local Authority decide who will look after your children.

Paying Inheritance Tax

If Inheritance Tax falls due on an Estate, then the Tax will need to be paid before any distribution can be made to the Heirs.

Famous Names who didn't do a good Job

I would like to take time here to point out a few famous names who didn't write their wishes down:

Pablo Picasso

Pablo Picasso died on the 8th April 1973, at the age of 91. He died without writing a Will. Source:- http://www.legalbot.co.uk/Celebrity-Intestacies-Part-5-featuring-Jimi-Hendrix-and-Pablo-Picasso-00021

Jimmy Hendrix

Died in 1970 at the age of 27, for 45 years his siblings fought over his Estate until they finally settled out of court in July 2015. (Source Sky News Aug 15,2015)

Bob Marley

Died in 1981 as at 2015 and 34 years later the Estate wrangling continues.

Source:- http://www.legalbot.co.uk/Celebrity-Intestacies-Part-3-featuring-Barry-White-and-Bob-Marley-00019

Barry White

When Barry White died on the 4th of July 2003, at the age of 58, he left behind 2 ex- wives, a long term lover and 9 children. (Source http://www.legalbot.co.uk/Celebrity-Intestacies-Part-3-featuring-Barry-White-and-Bob-Marley-00019)

Rik Mayall

When British Comedian Rik Mayall died in June 2014 he left a potentially huge tax bill of over £1M for his family as he had no Will. Source:- http://www.mirror.co.uk/3am/celebrity-news/rik-mayalls-family-face-huge-5556336

There are still other notable names that never had a Will such as former US President Abraham Lincoln and Martin Luther King Jr.

How about famous people who had Wills but failed to update them before the passed away?

Princess Diana

When Princess Diana died on August 31, 1997 she had a Will but had a 'Letters of Wishes' written alongside her Will but were deemed as not legally binding. Diana had wanted her God Children to receive items from her Estate however they did not receive anything close to what she intended as it was left up to her Executors to give what they decided as a 'Letters of Wishes' (in which she outlined her wishes) was deemed not legally binding.

Source:- http://www.legalbot.co.uk/Celebrity-Intestacies-Part-2-featuring-Heath-Ledger-and-Diana-Princess-of-Wales-00018

Heath Ledger

Died in January 2008 his Will had not been updated to write in his daughter that was born in 2005 nor was any provisions made for his daughter's Mom. His entire Estate went to his parents and siblings as per the original Will with nothing left to his daughter and her Mom.

Source:- http://www.legalbot.co.uk/Celebrity-Intestacies-Part-2-featuring-Heath-Ledger-and-Diana-Princess-of-Wales-00018

Guess what? You still have a chance to get it right. What is the best time to get this right? Now!

TRUST

We have the less famous cousin of the Will called a Trust. A Trust in essence is a Document that protects your Assets. A Trust is usually valid for

125 Years. It's also possible to write several Trusts to protect the Assets of an Estate.

A Trust is an arrangement where the Owner of Assets transfers their Assets to a Trustee and the Trustee holds the Assets on behalf of the Beneficiaries.

Here are the players in the Trust:

Settlor – The person who is putting their Assets into Trust.

Trustee – The Person who is in charge to managing the Trust.

Beneficiary – The Person who stands to benefit from the Trust.

Reasons for considering a Trust:

1- When your children are still minors.
2- In case you become incapacitated.
3- Protect the family's legacy for future generations.
4- Mitigate against inheritance tax.

There are always future instances that can sadly deplete your lasting legacy, such as Divorce, Bankruptcy, Care Home fees etc. Putting your Assets in a Trust will protect against this.

There is also another point to consider if you are Property Owners. That is if you are Joint Tenants or Tenants in Common. If you are Joint Tenants then you own the Property jointly. This also means that the entire Property passes to the other person if one dies. With Tenants in Common however, each person owns their half separately so each person can decide what happens to their half. A person can always get legal advice on how to change their Property Ownership.

It is of great importance that you sort out your wishes and lay out your instructions' suitably that if anything were to go wrong your family would be ok and your wishes would be honoured.

Reflection Points

Do you have a Will?

....

If you have a Will when was it last reviewed and does it need updating?

....

Do you now see the value of a Will and a Trust?

....

Are you ready to take action?

....

You must gain control over your money or the lack of it will forever control you.

Dave Ramsey
Financial Author

Chapter Eight

Watchmen

The Watchmen

In 2005 the Financial Services Industry which was previously regulated by several different regulators was taken over by a sole regulator, the Financial Services Authority (FSA). In 2013 the role was split and the Financial Conduct Authority (FCA) took over responsibility for consumer protection.

The main objectives of the regulator are:

1. Market confidence – maintaining confidence in the UK financial system;

2. Financial stability - contributing to the protection and enhancement of stability of the UK financial system

3. Consumer protection - securing the appropriate degree of protection for consumers; and

4. The reduction of financial crime - reducing the extent to which it is possible for a regulated

business to be used for a purpose connected with financial crime.

Financial Services Complaints Scheme

Step 1

In the first instance you complain in writing to the company involved, they in turn have eight weeks to respond to your complaint with a decision in regards to your complaint or advise you if more time is required to deal with your complaint. Please wait for this time to elapse before you progress your complaint to the next stage.

Step 2

If their final response to your complaint is not satisfactory or if the company rejects your complaint or you do not hear from them within eight weeks, then you can take your complaint to the **Financial Ombudsman Services**. The ombudsman service is a free, independent service for settling disputes between financial services companies and their customers.

It is important you contact the ombudsman service within six months of receiving a final response from the financial company, or the ombudsman service may not be able to deal with your complaint.

Step 3

If you do not accept the decision of the Financial Ombudsman Service and you have not used an independent complaints scheme, as a last resort you can take your case to court.

FSCS - Financial Services Compensation Scheme

The FSCS is the UK's compensation fund of last resort for customers of authorised financial services firms and arbitrator for financial services complaints. This means the FSCS may pay compensation if a firm is unable, or likely to be unable, to pay claims against it. This is usually because it has stopped trading or has been declared in default.

The FSCS covers business conducted by firms authorised by the Financial Conduct Authority

(FCA), the independent watchdog set up by government to regulate financial services in the UK and protect the rights of consumers.

European firms (authorised by their home state regulator) that operate in the UK may also be covered. However the FSCS does not cover the Channel Islands or The Isle of Man.

The FSCS protects:

- Deposits,

- Insurance policies,

- Insurance broking (for business on or after 14 January 2005), including connected travel insurance where the policy is sold alongside a holiday or other related travel (e.g. by travel firms and holiday providers) (for business on or after 1 January 2009);

- Investment business, and

- Home finance (for business on or after 31 October 2004).

As a fund of last resort there are limits to what the FSCS can do, and to the amounts of compensation the Scheme can pay. Financial Institutions usually provide leaflets outlining protection limits for deposit accounts.

YOUR ASSIGNMENT

1. Review your current Financial Position.

2. Go to www.barbaraanderson.net and download the 'Claim back your finances' tool. In each section put your current outlay, then with what you've learned, put in the amount you can trim back to. You can complete online or print off a copy in PDF and complete by hand.

Remember, what I have covered here with you is only some of the basics on money and should not be deemed as advice. Each person's situation is unique and we can only give you personal guidance once we have assessed your personal situation.

Managing On Nil Every Year

To get a **Complimentary Personalised Financial Game Plan** put in place contact us at: barbara@barbaraanderson.net

Tel: 07903 433791 or Fax: 08082801861

Try saving something while your salary is small; it's impossible to save when you begin to earn more.

Jack Benny Comedian

Managing On Nil Every Year

Final Word

"Strength does not come from winning. Your struggles develop your strengths. When you go through hardships and decide not to surrender, that is strength"

Finances might not be your area of expertise but if you take charge of your finances today you will be way ahead of most of the population tomorrow.

In closing I'd like to ask – Based on what has been covered here, what would you say is the most important thing for you right now?

Is it reviewing your financial situation, increasing your income or both?

People who soar are those who refuse to sit back, sigh and wish things would change.

They neither complain of their lot nor passively dream of some distant ship coming in. Rather, they visualize in their minds that they are not quitters.

They will not allow life's circumstances to push them down and hold them under.

I hope this has proven helpful.

I would love to hear from you with your positive feedbacks and to be your partner on your Financial Journey.

Please contact us at:

Email : barbara@barbaraanderson.net

Website: www.barbaraanderson.net

Twitter: @Barbara_9uk

Instagram: Barbara_9uk

Every time you borrow money you are robbing yourself of a future.

Nathan W Morris
Author & Personal Financial Expert

About the Author

In 1995 I stepped off a plane with lots of hope and big dreams. Travelling from a place known by many names, including poverty, to today educating families on finances. I have proven that indeed a 'journey of thousand miles begins with that first step'.

Belief is the start. I have worked in Financial Services for a number of High Street Financial Institutions, Management in Retail, as an Accountant and now an Entrepreneur in the Financial Services Sector.

As an Executive Vice President for a financial services company. I now focus on teaching families good financial practice.

It was the ability to reach into my soul and find the seed of belief, the belief that if the passion is strong enough and the vision large enough I can be an Achiever.

Today I am a Mother, an Advocate, a Developer and an Entrepreneur.

"Failure is not an option"

Whatever your views on **MONEY** you'd better:–

Accept it graciously

Earn it honestly

Invest it wisely

Own it legally

Understand it explicitly

Sometimes the best education is learned in the school of hard knocks!

The best thing money can buy is financial freedom.

Rob Berger
Forbes Berger

Book Barbara To Speak

Barbara is a Financial Educator improving the lives of many across the globe. She speaks at seminars, conference and workshops of themes like:

- Setting and achieving Financial Goals
- Planning for a better Financial Future
- Understanding Financial Products
- Creating Financial Impact
- Rising from the ashes

To book Barbara and give your event a powerhouse impact, contact us on:

E: Barbara@barbaraanderson.net

W: www.barbaraanderson.net

References

- Compound Interest Quote – Albert Einstein (www.goodreads.com)

- Rich Dad Poor Dad – Robert Kiyosaki

- Rule of 72 - en.wikipedia.org/wiki/Rule_of_72
- Problem have Solutions – (Song – You Will Know) Stevie Wonder

Recommend Resources

Here are some websites I have used and you may find useful:

- Inheritance Tax www.hmrc.gov.uk/inheritancetax

- Junior Individual Savings Account (ISA) www.gov.uk/junior-individual-savings-accounts/overview

- Financial Conduct Authority www.fca.gov.uk • Financial Ombudsman Services www.financial-ombudsman.org.uk

- Financial Services Compensation Schemes www.fscs.org.uk

- Government website www.gov.uk

- Association of British Insurers http://abi.bcis.co.uk/calculator/calculator.aspx

Managing On Nil Every Year

ZURIEL IT SOLUTIONS

Managing On Nil Every Year

PASSIONATE ABOUT BOOKS

Peaches Publications have over a decade of experience, knowledge and information in the book publishing industry.

Many authors get duped into spending thousand of pounds to bring their books to market.

We use our cost effective formula to help you go to print for the fraction of the price.

We help new authors bring their books to life by providing top quality services:

Digital publishing	Book publishing
Content	Amazon
Editing	Framework of books
Proof reading	Marketing
Book printing	Research
Sales	Print on demand
Kindle	Book coaching
Copyright	

www.peachespublications.weebly.com

Notes

Notes

Notes

Notes

Notes

Notes

Ten most important things I would like

....
....
....
....
....
....
....
....
....
....
....
....
....
....
....
....
....

Managing On Nil Every Year

Managing On Nil Every Year